Ek

An English Musical on the Life of

Shirdi Sai Baba

Usha Akella

Sterling Paperbacks

STERLING PAPERBACKS
An imprint of
Sterling Publishers (P) Ltd.
A-59, Okhla Industrial Area, Phase-II, New Delhi-110020.
Tel: 26387070, 26386209; Fax: 91-11-26383788
E-mail: mail@sterlingpublishers.com
www.sterlingpublishers.com

Ek
An English Musical on the Life of Shirdi Sai Baba
© 2012, Usha Akella
ISBN 978 81 207 6842 0

All rights are reserved.
No part of this publication may be reproduced, stored in a retrieval system or transmitted, in any form or by any means, mechanical, photocopying, recording or otherwise, without prior written permission of the author.

Printed in India
Printed and Published by Sterling Publishers Pvt. Ltd.,
New Delhi-110 020.

Contents

Characters 5

Introduction 7

ACT I: SHIRDI

Scene I
   Begin at the beginning   12

Scene II
   Under the neem tree   14

Scene III
   Shirdi village   15

Scene IV
   The feeding of Baba by Bayyaja Bai   21

ACT II: DWARKAMAI

Scene I
   God of the water lamps   24

Scene II
   The one within and without   31

ACT III: GRINDING! GRINDING! GRINDING!

Scene I
   Grinding! Grinding! Grinding!   36

ACT IV: WRATH OF THE FATHER; HEART OF A MOTHER

Scene I
    Garden work   50

Scene II
    Baba and the children   53

ACT V: *SABKA MALLIK EK*

Scene I
    Ramnavami and *Urs*   58

Scene II
    Qawalli   65

ACT VI: *EK*

Scene I
    I do not feel well here   68

Scene II
    Sabka Mallik Ek   71

Scene III
    Ek. Ek. Ek   72

    Glossary   74

    The Writing of Ek   77

Characters

Men:

Young Baba	:	16-year-old lad
Sai Baba	:	Saint of Shirdi; Adult, age 25–80
Young Tatya	:	Bayyaja Bai's son
Mahalsapati	:	Priest in Khandoba temple
Hemadpant	:	Author of Shri Sai Satcharitra
Bhagoji	:	Leper; prominent devotee
Das Ganu	:	Kirtan singer
Shama	:	School teacher
Abdul Baba	:	Prominent disciple; The 'crow' of Baba
Nanasaheb Chandorkar	:	Prominent devotee
Kote Patil	:	Bayyaja Bai husband
Chand Patil	:	Devotee from Dhoop village
Kakasaheb Dixit	:	Devotee
Vagne	:	Reader of Rama Vijaya
Saint Gagagir	:	Saint
Anandnath	:	Disciple of Akkalkot Maharaj
3 Shop keepers /Oil sellers		
1 *Radiwallah* (newspaper/ bottles/ bins seller)		
1 Cobbler		
Sagun	:	Chaiwallah

1 *Mithaiwallah*
1 Basket weaver
1 *Bhil*
2 muslim men : *Ali Mahomed, Ramaswami*
Nana's friends : *Vagne, Vijaya*
Nipathiranjana : *Guru*
Village Doctor : *Vaidya*
Cholkar and wife Ruku
Couple in miracle
Qawalli troupe
Drummers
Sword fighters

Women:
Young Lakshmi : *Favoured disciple of Sai*
Bayyaja Bai : *'Mother of Sai' and Tatya*
Radha Krishna Mai : *Prominent devotee*
1 Vegetable seller : *Bharathi*
2 village women : *Pushpa, Megha*
2 muslim women : *Amina, Zarin*
Mother of burnt child
Woman recovered from plague

Village Children:
Girls : *Lakshmi, Rani, Suchi, Puja, Bhavna, Preethi*
Boys : *Tatya, Kanha, Krishna, Vijju*

(Note on cast: Can be abbreviated and modified as per requirement)

Introduction

A worldwide phenomenon is the proliferation of godmen of varying qualifications and consumerist New Age religions that claim to make us all Gods easily. This age witnesses the erection of spiritual empires with vast wealth and power in contradiction to the fundamental spiritual value of poverty and abstinence of all kinds. The New Age religions recycle and package traditional wisdom for material gain and offer an inner la-la land, obliterating the primary requisite for spiritual progress — the presence of a genuine teacher or Guru; only one who has successfully traversed the path is fit to impart *Brahma Gnana*. Intellectual brilliance and oratory often masquerade as enlightenment and we have too often seen the crash and burn of such masters ending in scandal — economic, sexual and political. The resulting disappointment, sense of betrayal, chaos and shock is a spiritual epidemic. Left to sort through complicated psychological baggage with no solace, this is a terrible plight — an affliction that is profound. In this exploitative, confusing and vexing ambience, a handful of true masters still exert an authentic presence decades and centuries later. One of them is Sai of Shirdi. It is not an exaggeration to say that even today millions find an authentic master in him and a response to needs on all levels, even though he is no longer an embodied presence on earth.

Shirdi Baba is an enigma. His spiritual origins have been under debate for a century with no certain conclusions regarding his religion of birth. What is known for certain is that he was deeply soaked in the Sufi tradition and was knowledgeable of Vedanta. Neither the Hinduisation of the

Saint or the Islamic claim of his past will render the truth about his reality. No amount of culturalisation by one group can eradicate the presence of the opposing stream.

His universalism, tolerance and presence transcended narrow religious confirmation. What is striking to me was his acquiescence to be worshipped by devotees in their particular customs, and his ability to subvert traditional definitions and meld existing contradictory ones. God's religion was his. *Allah* and *Asanas*; *Ram* and *Rahim*; *Japa* and *Dhikr* — everything was on the same side of the fence. *Shraddha* (faith) and *Saburi* (patience) were the requisites, whatever the path. *Avaliya* or *Avatar* are sure to be immaterial terms to him. For one who saw himself as a servant of God, nomenclature is vanity. Surrender to God's will is essential to both the *bhakt* and the *mureed*; the absolute prerequisite for possible transformation. *Nafs* or *Maya* need to be overcome, whatever one's religious affiliation is.

Both Hemadpant and Abdul Baba recorded Baba's life and teachings. Though Hemadpant's *Charitra* has become another *Veda* for Hindus, Abdul Baba's recordings have not enjoyed the popularity of the former and need to be discovered en masse for his Sufi teachings. His original manuscript still lies in his descendant's home in Shirdi; it was published by Sterling titled: *Unravelling the Enigma: Shirdi Sai Baba in the light of Sufism* by Marianne Warren.

A remarkable outcome of Baba's presence in Shirdi was the simultaneous celebration of the *Urs* and *Ram Navami*. It is a tragedy that it has been discontinued. I felt his overriding message like Kabir was to breach the distance between both the communities. I think we lose his identity if we are hesitant to accept his evident Muslim/Sufi origin in dress, prayer and worship. It is remarkable that his embrace included all affiliations. His presence was his message.

I have no issue with hagiography. It has its uses as long as it does not morph the reality of the person venerated. One reality of Shirdi Sai was that he was a muslim fakir whose abode was a Hindu mosque! He was eccentric, explosive and harsh at times and yet had a boundless compassion like the universal mother. He was a penniless fakir recycling *dakshina* for common good and lived in a dilapidated mosque. A few rupees were found on his person at the time of his final *samadhi*. He begged for his food and had one *kafni* in the tradition of the Sufi fakirs — the one he wore. He promptly gave away clothes if any were offered to him. His *dhuni* could be the fire of the Zorastrianism, the *yagna* of the Hindu, or the Sufi *khaniqah*. The point of Baba is not what he was, a pointless quest for those who want to bind him, but of the impact of his presence that profoundly affects millions even today.

I am one of those million who has come under the magic of his grace and inner work. The idea to conceive a musical in English to convey his enigma and universalism began as a spark in December 2010. My intention in writing this play was to express the message of Baba in its complexity and to reach a younger English-speaking audience via theatre. It is a given that without his grace and guidance I could not have conceived the idea in the first place. I am deeply aware with humility that I am incapable of wholly understanding Baba. Talent must falter before that presence. There was the challenge of bringing the nuances of his story via the English medium. The task of rendering the profound layers of Eastern spiritual sensibility is beguiling. I constantly strive to meet that creative challenge in my works. This is only an attempt.

No task can be achieved without divine help filtering through human mediums. I am deeply grateful to all that made this happen.

ACT I:

SHIRDI

Scene I: Begin at the beginning

(Two children, a boy and girl watch a film of present day Shirdi on a background screen. The film presents a series of images of the bustling town as it is today. The children are dressed in traditional Indian clothes from the late 1800s — *pavada* or *parkar* for the girl and *dhoti-kurta* or *kurta-pajama* for the boy.)

Tatya : Shirdi has changed so much! How different life was back then — A sleepy village near Nasik. Nimgaon in the North. Rahata in the South.

We walked or ambled about in our bullock carts.

Lakshmi : Yes Tatya! No more than two hundred houses, two wells, the school, the *Khandoba mandir*, *Maruti mandir* and the *masjid*; no electricity and no roads!

Tatya : Prickly cactus at the village borders and the Lendi garden was just a handful of bushes and trees…

Lakshmi : And now… (she points to the screen)

Tatya : Now, all roads lead to Shirdi! Millions flock there. Our small unknown village is visited as much as Tirupathi.

Lakshmi : (smiling and reverential) Due to one. Our Baba!

Tatya : *Haan*. Our Baba. My Daada. A light for so many. He loved me more than his life. Remember Lakshmi, how Baba would say, *"I bring my men from any distance. I bring them to me. However distant even thousands of miles my people might be, I draw them to*

Shirdi like a sparrow with thread tied to its feet."

Lakshmi : So many sparrows are now flying home to our Shirdi. I miss those days Tatya. Remember how we flocked around Baba and he told us stories. I took him milk and bread everyday... he even played hop scotch with me.

Tatya : And marbles with me!

Lakshmi : And Das Ganu *chaacha* went about singing his *kirtans*...

(laughing) And you boys tied a bell to that cat's tail, stole mangoes and escaped from the classroom window...

Tatya : (smiles) We were naughty. We even played pranks on Baba before we knew he was our God, our everything... we called him the mad *fakir* and threw stones at him...

Lakshmi : And he never hurt us back. Just looked back at us with that bluish light in his eyes. And he was so kind. And his *Uddhi*... and the procession to the Chavadi...

(A shadow play of Baba in procession to Chavadi is seen on the backdrop.)

Those precious days won't be seen again... (she looks at the audience and stops). But Tatya, we should begin at the very beginning and tell these good people the story of the one who came from nowhere.

Tatya : And is everywhere!
(Curtains close)

Scene II: Under the neem tree

Setting : Twilight lighting. Neem tree. Line of shops, village well, masjid and village in foreground. The spotlight is on the neem tree.

A 16-year-old lad is in a meditative posture under it.

Backdrop : Village of Shirdi. Khandoba temple, Hanuman mandir and Chavadi.

(Voice-over) : Our story begins in 1868 perhaps. One cannot be so sure of the time when the story is timeless. A young lad of 16 years appeared under a neem tree in Shirdi, a tiny hamlet in Western India. So sweet was his presence, so dazzling his spiritual aura, it is said that the bitter leaves turned sweet.

Backdrop : Shadow play of Christ, Rama Krishna, Viveknanada and Whirling Dervish walking one by one in backdrop (from left to right).

(Voice-over) : Such ones have appeared in the course of history to alchemise ignorance to realisation, chaos to harmony and hate to love. They come as the most humblest of men; as carpenters or cowherds or like the lad of our story, as a penniless Fakir with no outward belongings. Living in our midst like ordinary men they do the most extraordinary things — they help us believe, God is here, God is here! In course of time, we are transformed like those neem leaves realizing bliss existed within, all along.

(Fade out light)

Scene III: Shirdi village

(Fade in light to bustling life in Shirdi village. Sun rising.)

Setting : Row of homes, village well, masjid that later becomes known as Dwarkamai, oil shops, cobbler and vegetable carts.

Create a village scene: Women with pots, women making *rangolis*, *chaiwallah*, *mithaiwallah*, cobbler, children playing hop scotch, basket weaver, iron smith etc.

Visible : Mahalsapati, Kote Patil, Bayyaja Bai, Tatya,
Characters   Lakshmi and village kids, Hemadpant, Das Ganu, Radha Krishna Mai, Shama, Bhagoji, Anandnath and Lakshmi.

(SONG–DANCE 1):
SHIRDI VILLAGE LIFE DANCE

Bayyaja Bai : *The Godavari is shimmering with anklets of light,*

Morning unveils her face and farewell to the night.

Radha Krishna Mai : *Wake! Arise! The eager rooster is crowing,*

Night gathers her dark skirts and is departing.

Kote Patil : *Our small village Shirdi will soon be another path,*

For one like Janeshwar, Shah Muni and Eknath.

Hemadpant : *The sun's riding his chariot fierce and fast,*

Last night's watchman's hoots won't last.

Bharathi	:	*For a golden glow is on the sky like a new bride,*
		Light your stove's fires, it's no time to hide.
All women	:	*We Shirdi women in bright nine yards and cholis,*
		Welcome Lakshmi devi with fine rangolis.
		(Women making *rangolis*.)
All	:	*Our ways are sure, our ways are set,*
		Keep to ourselves, to our own pockets,
		Crossing caste lines is a sin,
		First and foremost pure Brahmin,
		The rest follow, then the rest,
		Sonars, Sutars, Marathas, Lohar,
		Parit, Kumbhar, Chamar, Vadar,
		Marwadi, Mali, Bhil and Kolis.
		Like the varied colours of Holi!
Chaiwallah	:	*Chai garam, Chai garam, garam Chai to start your day… some spicy bakar vadda,*
		Your sleep will go away.
Kanha	:	*No school today mai… No school today…*
Mother	:	(dragging the kid) *Hai, what shall I do with you. Hai Hai!*
		(Shama walks by holding Vijju by the ear; Suchi, Lakshmi, Bhavna, Preethi, Puja, Krishna and Tatya follow).
		(Sleepy and yawning, the children chant multiplication tables, 2 ones are 2, 2 twos are 4…)
Shama	:	*For whom, for whom to run this school,*

		The villagers are no more than a pack of fools,
		The children want to play all day,
		Steal mangoes, slide on heaps of hay.
Hemadpant	:	Mahalsapati ji is hastening to wake Lord Khandoba,
		The temple bell's ringing, the aarthi is commencing.
		(Mahalsapati walks toward the Khandoba temple. Sound of aarthi and bells.)
Mahalsapati	:	(with *puja* plate)
		Worship our lord with bel and haldi, accept our navas,
		Worship our lord with kumkum and coconut, accept our fast,
		My Lord Khandoba arise!
		The one with the trident and fiery third eye!
Cobbler	:	I'll mend your heels,
		I'll mend your soles,
		I'll repair tears and holes,
		Wear my shoes!
		Upon a magic carpet!
		You'll float on air!
		Without a care!
All men	:	Unfasten the bullocks, fasten our turbans, walk on faster,
		The fields in green splendor await their masters.
Mithaiwallah	:	Mithai... srikhand... halwa... jilebi...
		These unbeatable puran polis.

Bayyaja Bai	:	*Oh! Pushpa and Radha bai… Let us hasten to the village well…*
Amina	:	*Waalekum Salaam Zarin behen* (Zarin and Amina embrace).
Oil sellers	:	*Rice, daal, spices and oil in til, peanut and gingelly,*
		Pay up first, not a drop without a rupee!
Raddiwallah	:	*Old paper! Bottles and bins! Sell me your unwanted things!*
Vegetable Seller	:	*My methi and paalak are fresh,*
		My tomatoes don't rot,
		My chilies are hot,
		My vangi are splendid like a king's robe,
		The beans with nimble fingers steal the show!
Basket weaver	:	*A basket for your earrings, a basket to store your rotis,*
		Baskets for all your needs; a basket to save your money.
Mahalsapati	:	*Shiva! Shiva!*
		Diseases daily like morning dew,
		These aches and pains,
		A never-ending refrain.
		(People come to him from all directions. He checks pulses and foreheads and sighs…) (Humour)
Das Ganu	:	*Don't forget! Tonight's the Harikatha of Seetha Ram,*
		Come all of you! Jai Hanuman!

Group	:	In Shirdi our lives are simple and sweet,
		Our hands are busy and so are our feet,
		Not far from Nasik, an unknown Hamlet,
		Our ways our sure, our ways are set.
		(Hindus to one side, Muslims on the other walking by toward the temple and masjid avoiding each other.)
		Our village deity Khandoba watches upon us,
		Our pace is slow never a rush,
		But someday the world will listen and see,
		Upon the map will sparkle our Shirdi.

(SONG–DANCE 2): LAVNI DANCE

Bhagoji	:	Outcast am I from this village scene,
		Gods are for those fortunate ones,
		Even God hides from me, I am unseen.
		(Dance ends with the villagers noticing the meditating figure under the tree and gradually they gather around looking at him. Dance and song subside to silence.)
		(Bhagoji hovers in the distance not mixing with the group.)
Bayyaja Bai	:	Whose blessed mother's son is he?
Mahalsapati	:	He seems to be a young yogi.
Kote Patil	:	How calm he is. How radiant!
Krishna	:	Who is he?
Tatya	:	Tugging Bayyaja Bai's pallu, "*Aai*, where has he come from?"

Bhavna	:	We've never seen him before! How beautiful he is! Like the moon!
Kanha	:	What's his name?
Preethi	:	Why is he sitting like that?
Suchi	:	Is he sleeping?
Rani	:	Has he walked here?
Puja	:	Where is his house?
Lakshmi	:	Is he going to live with us? He sparkles like a new coin.
Anandnath	:	This is a precious diamond. Mark my word, the shine from this one will illuminate the world. The destiny of Shirdi is about to change.

(Bhagoji moves forward to the yogi who reaches out his hand and takes his.)

(Sacred music and Fade out light)

Scene IV: The feeding of Baba by Bayyaja Bai

(Bayyaja Bai comes onto stage with a *tiffin* wrapped in cloth carried on her head.)

Kote Patil : By her side implores, "You have not eaten again Bayza. How long will you go hungry? What is this madness? Ever since that young yogi has come to Shirdi you have taken it upon yourself to feed him before eating. Who is he to you? He is not our son. Let's go home."

Bayyaja Bai : No ji. He is someone's son. Would she let him go hungry if she were here? You wait here. I will find him.

(She heads toward the jungle. Tatya enters and follows his mother.)

Kote Patil : Bayza, Bayza…

(He shakes his head, sighs and exits stage.)

She makes the gestures of someone looking for someone. Pulls aside branches, stumbles and clears leaves while calling for him. "Babu, Fakir Babu… Beta," she keeps repeating while looking about here and there. She espies him in the jungle and accosts him.

Bayyaja Bai : There you are! You cannot hide from me. Will a mother ever let her child go hungry? Why do you trouble me like this? No, no, never mind… trouble me all you like… that is what a child does, isn't it? I've made *sabudanyachi khichadi, roti, shrikand…*

(Baba is quiet, standing still and looking into the distance. Like a mother she cajoles him to eat watching in adoration as she feeds him. He silently accepts her love.)

Bayyaja Bai	:	"Whose son are you re? Where are you from? Won't your mother miss you?" Here you are again seeing things we can't see. (She looks in the direction he is looking and can't see anything). She sighs, "I keep chattering like the *chatak* bird. You keep silent like the early morning sky only radiant with light. You don't worry about food, alright. I am here. As long as I am here you will not go hungry. There is no worry." She wipes tears sentimentally and oblivious to the irony says, "You are not alone. We in Shirdi won't leave you alone."
Baba	:	(smiling gently at the irony) "*Allah Mallik*"!
		She wraps up the tiffin and makes her way out.
		(Gradual fade out light while she leaves.)
(Voice-over)	:	The young lad stayed in Shirdi for three years and disappeared. He returned a year later with the marriage procession of Chand Patil of Rahata. Mahalsapati, the village priest hailed him as '*Sai*' and henceforth he became known as Sai Baba. He was recognised as the very same young yogi first spotted under the neem tree.
		Gradually, he settled in an old masjid that he called Dwarkamai. Initially, he attended to the villagers like a *hakim*. He begged for his food from five houses. He had no belonging except for a *chilim*, tin pot and *choli*. He burned a *dhuni* day and night and distributed the Uddhi from the dhuni that had healing properties. He exhibited his mastery over nature, healed the sick and read the innermost thoughts of people. He knew the past, present and future of anyone he met. He shunned no one. Still, no one knew his origins. His ways were mysterious.

ACT II:

DWARKAMAI

Scene I: God of the water lamps

(Curtains open)

(Dwarkamai has 3 niches, railing on two sides, inner room and outer room, *kolamba*, *Tulsi* plant, dhuni, chilims and lamps. The masjid has flags on the outside.

Baba is reclining in the inner room by the railing. His hand rests on a brick. The burning Dhuni is visible. Baba puts logs in the fire. Baba distributes uddhi to some who come. He settles down and begins to grind some wheat. He concentrates on the task. Bhagoji is with him attending to him. Radha Mai is cleaning the masjid. Abdul is sweeping outside. Radha Mai is seen moving a brick carelessly while re-arranging things.)

Abdul : Oh Radha Mai. How many times have I told you? Be careful with that brick and how you handle it. Baba treasures it as his life.

(Shaking her head uncomprehendingly. She dusts it carefully and puts it back.)

Radha Mai : (to the audience) A worthless brick is a treasure in this masjid and jewels and wealth are not glanced at. While the world sleeps at night, he is awake. Everything is upside down for this Deva. And somehow it make things right.

Abdul : There you go muttering under your breath again.

Mahalsapati : (Passing by with Shama and Hemadpant looks at Baba, continues to walk and then goes back again.)
Why is this Baba grinding wheat?

Hemadpant : (Shakes his head in the negative. Mahalsapati, Shama and Hemadpant stop and watch curiously.)

Shama : Mahalsapati ji, have you and I understood a single thing that he does? He speaks with another alphabet and we fascinated are pulled to him like the earth to the sun. Have you observed his signs by the Hanuman mandir? (scratching his head) I tell you that language is from another *loka*. I have not heard it on this earth.

(Lakshmi and Tatya enter.)

Lakshmi : Baba, what are you doing? Why have you taken this task upon you?

Tatya : Daada, let us bring someone to help you.

(running to the village and shouting) Baba is grinding wheat.

Pushpa : (enters with Bhavna, Preethi, Puja, Suchi, Vijju, Krishna and Kanha) Aay! What is he upto now? This Deva's ways are unknown to anyone. (rushes off calling), "Bayyaja Bai!"

Lakshmi : Baba, what are you doing? Why are you grinding? Shall I help you?

(Tatya and Lakshmi go up to Baba. The kids flock around him. The villagers slowly gather and watch him.)

Bayyaja Bai : Baba, *hato beta*... We are here to help you. (She pushes through the crowd of kids and forcibly pushes Baba away and takes the handle.)

(Baba yields.)

Pushpa, Amina, Bharathi... give me a hand.

(The women grind merrily and cheerfully. When they are done, they gather the wheat, distribute it in four heaps and are about to go home.)

	(Baba till then who is about doing his work notices this and is enraged.)
Baba :	Have you gone mad? Is this your father's property? Is this your wheat? (softening his tone) No… no… no… take this wheat and go to the village border and sprinkle it there…
Women :	But Baba…
Mahalsapati :	Baba, how are we to understand your ways…
Baba :	Go… Go… Go. (He motions the villagers to go.)
	(He goes back to his Dhuni.)
Hemadpant :	(Writes something in his notebook). To the audience:
	This reminds us of Kabir who seeing a woman grinding corn said to his Guru, Nipathiranjana, "I am weeping because I feel the agony of being crushed in this wheel of worldly existence like the corn in the hand-mill."
	Nipathiranjana replied, "Do not be afraid; hold fast to the handle of knowledge of this mill, as I do; and do not wander far away from the same but turn inward to the Centre, and you are sure to be saved."
Mahalsapati :	Mark my words Dabolkar ji… this Baba's actions will be known in time. No lie ever escapes his lips… in his actions are the hidden ways of God…wait and see…
	(Villagers slowly disperse and return back to their work.)
	(Baba alights the stairs with Bhagoji's help.)

		(**Famous Scene** of Baba begging from house to house with *chaddhar* on his head in the village. He extends his *jholi* and *tumrel* for food.)
Baba	:	*Mai Bhakrian. Aai, Bhikshaam Dehi. Bhikshaam Dehi. Mallik Tere Bale Kare.*
		Allah Mallik. Allah Mallik. Sabka Mallik Ek Hai.
Kids	:	(the children tug at his *khafni*) "Baba Baba."
Kanha	:	Baba play with us today. You promised us yesterday.
		(Baba carries Krishna fondly.)
Tatya	:	Come Baba. I will win this time.
Suchi	:	No! Baba promised to play hop scotch with us.
Rani	:	You boys are always taking him away from us. (She pushes Kanha. He pushes back.)
Bhavna		
Preethi		
Puja	:	(Join in the fight.)
Lakshmi	:	Baba, tell them it's our turn.
Baba	:	*Accha accha.* (He separates the kids and makes peace.) Let's play together.
		(Baba stops and plays marbles with the kids. While this is going on the oil sellers gang up.)
Oil seller 1	:	There he is begging his morning round and then he will come here asking us for oil. His eyes glitter and glow. I can't look him in the eye. Once I tried and felt he looked

so deep into me I drowned in those eyes. My mind became as still as one of those butchered cows of Bhaliya's... I can't say "No" to him and he is never going to pay me back.

Oil seller 2 : All day "Allah Mallik" "Allah Mallik" This muslim fakir is a sly fox.

He knows our scriptures too like a learned Brahmin... He asked Keshava the potter to chant the *Vishnusahasranama*... no one can hold a debate about the *Bhagavat* or *Gita upadesh* without looking like a fool in front of him... I heard that he pricked the ego of Nanasaheb Chandorkar... He was quiet as a cat that had its tail stepped on after Baba caught him on the Gita... Is he Hindu or Muslim?

Oil seller 3 : Who knows... the walls of the masjid are silent about this. And that Mahalspati... first bars him from the Khandoba mandir and then (pauses dramatically) becomes his most ardent devotee.

He has taken to sleeping in the masjid with Tatya and swears Baba is Khandoba. Shiva Allah! Shankara Fakir! And our Khandoba on the hill is silent about all this...

Oil seller 1 : Do you know what that masjid is called now? Dwarkamai. Krishna's own name for a Muslim *dargah*... These people of Shirdi have gone mad my brother.

I don't want to support his prayers if he is a Muslim. If he is really God why doesn't he make his own oil. (His expression changes as it begins to dawn on him.) *Bhai log*, I have an idea. What is he going to do if we tell him there is no oil, huh? What is he going to do? Is oil going to pour from heaven? (Laughter)

Oil seller 3	:	(laughing) Let him use water today. The God of the water lamps!
Baba	:	Allah Mallik! (Baba comes up to them and stretches forth his tin pot.) Oil for my Dwarkamai. My Dwarkamai has work to do tonight.
Oil seller 2	:	(lying)... Oh Baba! We would be so glad to give you oil. Don't we do so everyday? But today there is none.
Oil seller 1	:	None.
Oil seller 3	:	Not a drop.
Oil seller 2	:	Aah (shaking his head sadly). Why don't you ask Allah to provide today? (sneering)
Baba	:	(smiling unperturbed) Allah Mallik! He walks back toward the Dwarkamai. (The oil sellers follow him.)
Suchi	:	Lakshmi, Preethi, come... (all the girls hold hands and follow).
Tatya	:	(to Bayyaja Bai...) Aai, Aai, the shopkeepers have refused to give oil to Baba. (She shakes her head and follows.)

(The villagers slowly flock and follow him to the Dwarkamai.)

(Bayyaja Bai and the women crack their knuckles at the shopkeepers. They dismiss them off arrogantly and stomp on.)

(Baba unconcerned, walks toward the Dwarkamai. He climbs the steps. First, he offers a roti to the dhuni and then puts the food in the Kolamba for anyone to partake of it. Looks about. Picks up a tin pot of water. Raises it, drinks some and forcefully spits it back in the pot. He then takes the pot and pours it into the lamps one by one.) (Dim lights)

(The lamps begin to burn.)

(Dwarkamai lights up in a blaze.)

(The shopkeepers are dismayed. The people raise a cry):

Jai Sai Baba!

(Lightening and thunder.)

(People run helter-skelter. Parents call out for kids. Fear and panic.)

Villagers : Help us Baba. Help us Baba.

(The children hide behind him.

Baba raises his finger to the sky and commands the storm to stop.)

Baba : "Stop! Enough! Abate now! Calm down! Let these people be.

Gradual cessation of thunder and lightning.

Villagers crowd around him in devotion and adoration.

(Fade out light)

(Voice-over) : *Soon after Baba's grinding and sprinkling of the wheat, Shirdi was spared from the cholera raging in the district. The mad fakir began to win hearts by his miracles and compassion. He was ever present to their difficulties and woes. Many came in curiosity, some in doubt and some in faith. But all left with a change of heart, convinced of an inexplicable divinity.*

Scene II: The one within and without

(Curtains Open)

Setting : (This act presents a series of *leelas* of Baba in brief flashes. The stage is dark. First, a spotlight on the Dwarkamai. Baba is with his devotees in the masjid looking in the direction of where the scene is about to unfold. He is concerned and following the actions there. He is lost in thought not paying attention to the devotees who call him and remark to each other):

Devotees : He is somewhere else! He cannot hear us! He is here and somewhere else!

(Fade out spotlight)

(Fade in spotlight on another corner on stage):

Miracle 1:

Nana : (Makes the actions of one climbing and greatly exhausted. He exclaims to his friend):

Water. Water. I can climb no longer. The Devi temple is still a way to go. I need water. I don't think I can reach there. I am parched. Water.

Friend : (concerned) I have none my friend. We drank the last drop. Where on this hill can I find water. Let us go back.

Nana : (sitting down and exclaiming) If Baba were here he would surely give me water.

Friend : (irritated) Your Baba is not here. Of what use is it calling him. Of what good is that. Save your breath.

(Baba to devotees, concerned):

My Nana is thirsty. My Nana is on Harischandra Hill. He needs water. Now. Now. He needs water. He needs a handful of water to go on. He raises his hand in blessing. (Devotees look on bewildered.)

Bhil : (A hill tribesman appears)

Nana : Ayy bhai. Water. I need water.

Bhil : What? You ask for water? Under the very rock you sit on!

Nana : (Nana and friend move the rock and ecstatic and relieved Nana drinks a palm full of water.)

(Fade out light)

Miracle 2:

(Fade in light)

(Cholkar, a poor man and his wife are praying to Baba's photograph)

Cholkar : Baba, by your grace I have passed the department examination and got the permanent job. As promised I will come to Shirdi and distribute sugar candy and fall at your feet. Please help me. Please be patient Baba. As you know I do not have the means now.

(To his wife)

Ruku, from today, I will give up sugar in my tea. Keep the money saved from this aside. In time I will be able to go to Shirdi with Baba's grace.

Ruku : (She accepts the money with devotion): All will be well by Baba's grace. Surely, you will go to Shirdi.

(Fade out)

(Fade in light at Dwarkamai)

(Cholkar walks into Dwarkamai. He prostrates at Baba's feet.)

Baba : (to Shama) Shama, give this Cholkar tea fully saturated with sugar.

Cholkar : (overcome and hugging him) Baba... Baba... you know it all.

Miracle 3:

(Spotlight on Dwarkamai):

(A couple comes in carrying a boy with convulsions. They have lost hope and plead with Baba for help. He administers the Uddhi gently and cares for the boy. The boy sits up cured.)

(Fade out)

(Voice-over Baba) : *Remember this well:*

Whosoever steps into this Dwarkamai, irrespective of their status, will get happiness. His suffering comes to an end. This mother is very benevolent. The wretched and miserable will rise to joy and happiness as soon as they climb the steps of Dwarakamai.

The place where the doors are open for all people regardless of caste, community and creed, for accomplishing Dharma, Artha, Kama, and Moksha is called 'Dwaraka.'

(Curtains Close)

ACT III:
GRINDING! GRINDING! GRINDING!

Scene I: Grinding! Grinding! Grinding!

(DANCE–SONG 3)
(Frozen scene of all villagers)

Hemadpant	:	(Writing *Sai Satcharit* looks up)
		What does grinding wheat have to do with cholera?
		Hmmm... Someone ought to write these Sai Leelas.
Chorus	:	Grinding... Grinding... Grinding...
		Always, always calm and smiling...
		As fierce as a storm in rage,
		As calm as an empty stage,
		Grinding... Grinding... Grinding...
		Everyday he is grinding... never, never revealing!
Mahalsapati	:	He wandered in, one kafni upon his back,
		Yet not the look of one who lacked.
		(Musing/Counting on his fingers one by one):
		Chilim, tumrel, dhuni, satka, kafni, jholi
		(Shaking his head in the negative)
		Yet not the look of one who lacked.
		With ease I called him Sai,
		He became my all, my ma baap bhai.
Tatya	:	God is all one needs he lives and shows,
		Holds darbar in an old masjid with a divine glow.

Villagers : *He sees my past!*
He knows my thoughts!
He offers food to all in that pot!
(Beggar seen helping himself from it)
He suffered for me!
He cured my child!
He cures the blind!
I saw his intestines on a tree!
Who is he? Who is he? Who is he?
His ways are a mystery!

Mahalsapati : *A fool! A fool! I barred the Lord's way in,*
When the temple's within,
And now I know he is what I yearned for.
My Guru, he took me in and opened the door,
At first he didn't sleep upon the floor!
Seven feet high,
Almost in the sky,
Like a paper boat, a bed
Wobbling with flimsy rags instead!

Tatya : *A bed! A bed with burning lamps,*
Wonders of wonders, a divine stamp,
It left us all scratching our heads!
Who but the Lord can sleep on such a bed!

Villager : *He is not logical!*

Villager : *Nor dialectical!*

Villager : *Nor comprehensible!*

Villager : *His actions are invisible!*

Villager	:	*He is dependable!*
Villager	:	*Available!*
Villager	:	*Reliable!*
Villager	:	*Incredible. Calm. Peaceful. Wise. Liberal!*
Villager	:	*Self-contained!*
Villager	:	*Self-absorbed!*
Villager	:	*An ancient sage!*
Villager	:	*Durvasa's rage!*
Villager	:	*Cares not for honor or dishonor!*
Villager	:	*His soul is clear as a mirror!*
Chorus	:	*Grinding, Grinding, Grinding!* *What is he grinding?* *Our sins, our losses, our pride,* *The hidden dirty side,* *He leaves the best for us,* *Grinds the rest to dust.*
Bhagoji	:	*My friend, my family, the only one who accepts me.* *Rich and poor are the same, he cooks us all feasts.* *Do you know of anyone who'd take your pain,* *Suffer your sins and life's ill gotten gains?*
Chorus:		*Grinding... Grinding... Grinding...* *No ordinary fakir begging, begging, begging!*
Nana	:	*Nanasaheb is my name.* *Knowledge is my fame.*

                    Versed in Vedic lore,
                    Ancient scriptures galore,
                    Thought I knew it all,
                    Pride comes before the fall!

Five women   :   Begging daily door to door,
                    Never asking for more,
                    A single kafni on his self,
                    With glances that melt
                    The hardest cores...
                    He never asks for more,
                    He begs to relieve you of your sin,
                    And holds darbars, the king of kings.

Bayyaja Bai   :   Who is he?
                    The Lord as well as my own family,
                    Calls me his sister of many births,
                    I have not one son, I say, but two... this is the truth.

Woman   :   From a fire he saved my child,
                    In terror and fear I was wild,
                    In his Dhuni here he placed his hand,
                    No one understands, No one knew,
                    There she was safe, fresh as dew.

Bhagoji   :   (Tenderly bandaging his arm)
                    The chance to tend to his needs,
                    Who'd think this would be my destiny,
                    Once abandoned and shunned,
                    Today I walk with the holiest one.

Shama	:	*He sometimes speaks in jest and fun,*
		Raises a storm, abates it and simply done,
		Pinches my cheek, calms me down,
		Wipes away my sulks and frowns,
		"72 generations Shama," he says,
		I've known you beyond this time and day."
Villager	:	*Sometimes passive. Sometimes bold.*
		Silent as the sea, never leaves the threshold,
		Yet his ashram is the world,
		He knows what's happening everywhere,
		While sitting on his humble chair.
Das Ganu	:	*God's own... the Rajadhirajah,*
		Sri Sai Sat Chit Ananda.
Muslim	:	*Allah's own dhoot,*
		The embodiment of truth,
		Ya Mallik! Ya Nur!
Villager 1	:	*No need to meditate!*
Villager 2	:	*Ruminate!*
Villager 3	:	*Reiterate!*
Villager 4	:	*Levitate!*
Villager 5	:	*Suffocate!*
Rani	:	(The kids showing various yogic poses. Comically tottering and falling):
		Don't twist your limbs in agony,
Tatya	:	*Stand on your head, get all giddy,*
Suchi	:	*No Garudasana!*

Bhavan	:	*No Virabhadrasana!*
Preethi	:	*No Dhanurasana!*
Puja	:	*No Konasana*
Lakshmi	:	*No Trikonasana!*
All kids	:	*No Sirsasana* (They prop up little Krishna on his head and all tumble down laughing.)
Mahalsapati	:	*The easiest way is his way,* *Sukhasana! Sainatha!* *Surrender, surrender, surrender!* *Get rid of your ahamkara.*
Woman	:	*My plague he took on as his own,* *Raging fevers and bodily blows.*
Oil seller	:	*The fire's always burning!*
Oil sellers	:	*Burning! Burning! Burning!* *Something's always burning!*
Chorus	:	*A kindly, kindly burning!* *Our sins, our sins are burning!*
Kanha	:	*This holy Uddhi is what I had,* *It drove away fits and all things bad,* *This Uddhi drives away your sins,* *This Uddhi combats afflictions!*
Villager	:	*Barren, waxen, plague and malaria,* *Fits, starts, aches, pains and asthama,* *He has the divine sanction to cure,* *Nectar is his word, undiluted, pure,*

The dead rise like they've just been asleep,
Like a forgotten promise to keep.

(All the kids mimic the actions above.)

Man : *Seen and unseen demons in my brain*
He sieved my soul, till my soul I gained.

Abdul : *Words like pearls, words like fire,*
Is he the hidden one who pulls the wires?

(The kids play act a puppet show.)

Zarin : *A perfect avaliya from the grace of Allah!*

Amina : *What need of other maulvis and messiah!*

Nana : *Not one that hoards and holds,*
Yet without battering a lid and bold,
May ask again, again for dakshina.
Ask for you to give what you forget,
Makes you give till your debt is met.

Villagers : *He grinds our sins!*
He grinds afflictions!
He grinds ignorance!
Accepts repentance!
He clears the path!
He shows the way!
No seven devotional baths a day!

Grinding! Grinding! Grinding!
In his self-abiding.

		It's all the same to him,
		Devotees and doers of sin,
		His heart's filled to the brim.
Nana	:	A never-ending solace,
		God's very own face,
		He is here to take your load,
		Whatever your religion or mode,
		Of worship… it's all the same to him,
		Different signs on God's royal road,
		No distinction between diamonds and stone,
		Rich or poor we are all his own,
		He won't leave you alone,
		Up high mountains,
		Down sharp bends.
		Till your journey's end,
Villagers	:	Grinding! Grinding! Grinding!
		There's a new awakening,
		In Shirdi… the sun is ever shining!
Tatya	:	Don't dare leave Shirdi,
		While he is sleeping,
		No permit! No leaving!
		I did it once… what a dunce…
		My horse lost control,
		I ran back to Shirdi the very next day.
		Will never try to sneak away!
Hemadpant	:	A foolish soul, I had my plans,
		I thought I knew who was my clan,

                  I charted each step of my life,
                  I dreamt only of kids, job and a wife.
                  A sacred perfume caught me in its charm,
                  The scent of God's own, begging for alms.

Mahalsapati : *Three nights and three days upon my lap,*
                  His breathing stopped! Not just a nap!
                  "Watch over me! Three days and three nights,"
                  The vermin stormed the masjid for a fight,
                  I forbid them to touch his holy frame,
                  On his word death and life are the same,
                  Beyond this body and this flesh,
                  Beyond the obvious mortal mesh,
                  He woke up glorious as the sun wakes,
                  From a voyage across an unknown lake.
                  He is more than just the body that died –
                  The ABSOLUTE ETERNAL SELF inside!

Das Ganu : *I threw away my master plan laughing,*
                  At these holy feet I found my true soul's calling,
                  True Bhakti he extracted from this clay,
                  In holy Shirdi, I am here to stay.

                  No mantra, no tantra, no need of thirthyatra,
                  No holy dips in Prayag or Ganga,
                  All sacred rivers are here in Shirdi,
                  At his holy feet he purifies you and me.

                  (Touches his feet. Prayag water flows from his feet. Can be shown on screen.)

Villagers	:	*He is my Rama!*
		My Krishna!
		My Panduranga!
		My Vithala!
		Our Khandoba!
		Dattatreya!
		Dhoot of Allah!
		All the saints bow to him!
		My Akkalakot Maharajah!
		Meher Baba!
		Gajanan Maharajah!
		Again Kabir has come!
Chorus	:	*Grinding! Grinding! Grinding!*
		Nature's a salve, obedient in his fist,
		Grinding cholera to bits and bits!
		Grinding! Grinding karmic debts!
		Disease, death and destiny,
		Grinding! Grinding inner misery!
		Who is he? Who is he? Who is he?
		His ways are a mystery.
Nanasaheb Chandorkar	:	*Hear! Hear! Live up to any holy vows,*
		Baba says, "One reaps what one sows."
		Square up on your old debt and dealings,
		No escape from deceit, greed and freewheeling,
		One suffers what he does to others,
		Listen sisters, brothers, fathers and mothers!

Mahalsapati :	*Maya has no hold on him,*
	Nor family, wealth or kin,
	Such ones come upon the earth,
	To uphold the laws of Dharma,
	When Dharma declines,
	Never fear, Never mind…..
	The saints take birth,
	To lighten burdens on the earth,
	Maya has no hold on him!

(DANCE-SONG 4):

The Dance and defeat of *Maya/Kalyuga*
(Music and dance only. No lyrics)

(End dance)

(Scene ends with all bowing and Baba in posture of benediction.)

(Light on Dwarkamai)

(Villagers touching his feet. Villagers garlanding him.)

(Freeze characters)

Hemadpant :	*Grinding! Grinding! Grinding!*
	Nature's a salve, obedient in his fist,
	Grinding cholera to bits and bits!
	Who is he? Who is he? Who is he?
	His ways are a mystery,
	The purnavatar of this age,
	The Purna Guru! Our maa baap bhai,
	Sri Rajadhiraja Sat Chit Ananda Sai.

Dwaraka here again with our Lord Hari,
Lifts our burdens, our mother Sai,
A father's wrath, a mother's heart,
Our own Karuna Mai!
The one without name or form,
The one within a leaf and storm,
The sacred Nirgun is Sagun now,
Miracles of miracles,
Don't ask me how!

In his heart all things melt into one,
All human definitions come undone.

Tonight to the chavadi!
The holy abode of Sad Guru Shirdi Sai!
Tonight to the chavadi!

(Writing in his notebook.)

Chorus	:	(softly) *Grinding, Grinding, Grinding.*
		(Chavadi Procession: Baba is lead with fanfare from the Masjid to the Chavadi. One devotee holds an umbrella over his head. One strews rose petals. Dancing. Trumpets.)
(Voice-over Baba)	:	*You need not go far, or anywhere in search of Me. Barring your name and form, there exists in you, as well as in all beings, a sense of Being or Consciousness of Existence. That is Myself. Knowing this, you see Me inside yourself as well as in all beings. If you practice this, you will realise all pervasiveness and thus attain oneness with Me.*

(Curtains Close)

ACT IV:

WRATH OF THE FATHER; HEART OF A MOTHER

Scene I: Garden work

(Baba draws water from the well. He pours it into his pot. He carries it to the garden at Booty wada, which eventually becomes the Samadhi *mandir*, and waters plants and trees. People walking about touch his feet, take his blessings, offer to help, he refuses...)

(Radha Krishna Mai is seen sweeping the street around the masjid.)

Baba : No, no. One should do one's own work.

(Tatya and Lakshmi follow with garden tools and work as well.)

Mahalsapati : Baba you tend our souls like this garden. Weed out the poisonous, nourish us with your light and make us bloom into something beautiful. The people in Shirdi have changed since your coming. The women sing your leelas while cleaning and cooking on the way to the fields and back...

Hemadpant : No evil can touch the borders of this village. Ghosts and ghouls are scared to enter for they know that God lives here... Baba, even our Shirdi cows know when you are near... they perk their ears and come to attention.

Baba : What things will flower from bones here... (Mahalsapati does not comprehend.) People will come to Shirdi like ants upon ants.

Saint Gagagir : Blessed is Shirdi, that it got this precious
(passing by) jewel! In this heap of dung!

(Enter Das Ganu doing Kirtan followed by children.)

(Enter Shama as if from a journey.)

Baba	:	Shama, how was your thirthyatra? *Khub maza kiya?* Ayodhya, Kashi, Gaya... *sab theek tak*... how was Gaya?
Shama	:	(overcome) Baba, as you said you were ahead of me. Bursts into tears of happiness.
Mahalsapati	:	(not comprehending but nodding knowingly) Lo! One more *leela*!
Lakshmi	:	Shama chacha, what happened in Gaya?

(All walking back to the masjid.)

Shama	:	Before I left, I came to Baba for his *darshan*. And he told me he would be ahead of me after Prayag and Kashi. We stayed in the Gaya Dharmasala; after a good night's rest our guide took us to his house. I stepped in, and the first thing I see is a big and beautiful portrait of Baba. Right in front, as if to welcome me. I was so overcome and started crying and trembling. And can you believe it? I had given that *Gayawallah* that picture twelve years ago when he came to Shirdi. We remembered it all... Baba says whatever you give comes back to you. And if we give God anything it comes back a hundred fold.
Baba	:	(smiling) *Shraddha* and *Saburi*. These are the coins my Mallik likes to receive most.
Tatya	:	Baba, better than money!
Shama	:	I will take your leave now Baba and come to the masjid in the evening. (He exits.)
Hemadpant	:	Mahalsapati, do you know the same thing happened to me. Baba says seeing a picture of him is a *darshan* of him. He is organising everything in the universe, even the tremor

of a leaf or the boldness of a wave... not a thing is unknown to him... everything in this world is like a vast puzzle... in time, it all fits.

I had a dream of Baba dressed like a *Sanyasi* who said he would eat with us that day. I was overjoyed and doubtful at the same time... Baba does not eat at anyone's place, but again his word is never false. Isn't it Mahalspati ji? I told my wife this news and she said, "From Shirdi? Baba will come to Bandra from Shirdi? To our humble abode? To eat parched rice and roti!" She looked at me as if my senility had begun.

We made our preparations. Spread out the leaves, made the rangoli marks around them, we started serving food. We kept the door open. No sign of him. Disappointed we closed the door. I offered the *naivadya* to Vaishwadeva and Krishna Bhagvan and then... (he pauses dramatically) there were footsteps heard and a knocking of the door. There were two *mussalman*... I thought I was dreaming... one of them gave me a packet wrapped in newspaper. I was bewildered... seeing that we were about to eat, the gentleman said he would explain all later... I unwrapped the packet and... it was Baba's picture. I placed it on the seat we had reserved for Baba... I met Ali Mahomed nine years later who told me how he got the picture. But that story is for another afternoon... there are hundreds of leela's... when can one stop? (He looks heavenwards.)

Mahalsapati : Baba's words come out true to the letter. Ganu, now your overflowing heart will pour out more kirtans and more and more will come to know of our Baba.

Scene II: Baba and the children

(Enter kids with Das Ganu)

Kids : Ganu chacha, Ganu chacha teach us a song. Chalo…

(They settle in the masjid; Baba is sitting on a rock with his right leg over the left. Ganu teaches kids the following song. Devotees are worshipping Baba in the way they like. Washing His feet. Garlanding. Fanning. Pressing His feet. Massaging.)

(DANCE-SONG 5):
(BHAJAN)

sai ram, sai ram, bolo sai ram
shirdiwale sai ram
bada pyara tera naam

sab dukh door karnewale
sab ko rah dikhlanewale
shanti sabko denewale
sharan me sab ko lenewale
baba tujhe pranam
bada pyara tera naam

man ki shakti badhanewale
gyan ka phool khilanewale
pyar ke jot jalanewale
naman mera o shirdiwale
baba tujhe pranam
bada pyara tera naam

sai ram, sai ram, sai ram, Shirdiwale sai ram

(Composed by Vani Arvind; Austin, Texas)

Baba	:	Be wherever you like, do whatever you choose, remember this well that all that you do is known to me. I am the Inner Ruler of all and seated in their hearts. I am the Controller—the wire-puller of the show of this Universe. I am the mother —the origin of all beings. All the insects, ants, the visible, movable and immovable world is my Body or form.
Tatya	:	Haan Baba, you always teach us that... do you know what we've been doing since the morning. We've been acting a play on the two lizard sisters... can we show you Baba?
Baba	:	(eagerly) Haan Tatya... show me, show me.
Krishna	:	(wrapping a cloth on his head) I am Baba. (all laughing) Allah Mallik!
		(Kanha and Bhavna fan him.)
Tatya	:	(addressing Krishna) Baba, why is that lizard twitching and swirling?
Suchi	:	(donning lizard mask; twitching and whirling.)
Kanha	:	Because her sister is on her way from Aurangabad.
Tatya	:	Sister? Lizards have sisters? Aurangabad? (shakes his head disbelievingly)
Rani & Puja	:	(Come in galloping like a horse and Preethi acts as a *tangewallah*. They stop. She opens a bag of grains. Lakshmi emerges wearing a lizard mask. She goes up to the other lizard and they dance merrily, swirling

and whirling. Krishna smiles benignly and raises hand in blessing.)

(All clap. The children flock to Baba and sit on his lap.)

Lakshmi : Baba, wait. I have something for you. Don't move.

(She brings back milk and bread. Offers it to Baba. He accepts it. Blesses her and gives it to a dog that comes by. Pats it lovingly.)

Lakshmi : Baba, how could you do that? I brought it for you so lovingly!

(Baba goes up the stairs to the second level.)

Baba : Lakshmi beti. Know that all beings are one. Appeasing that dog's hunger satisfies me. He who feeds the hungry is most dear to me. *Annadaan* is the most important of charity. Feed the hungry first before you feed yourself. Remember me before eating.

(Enter Shama in agony supported by villagers.)

Shama : Baba, help me!

Villagers : A snake has bitten him Baba. He refused any other medicine and insisted we bring him here.

Shama : Help me Baba. (He starts to ascend the stairs.)

Baba : (All of a sudden enraged and out of control.)

Get down! I say Get down! Get down!

Shama : But Baba...

Baba	:	Get down! Now! Do as I say! You evil one! Down! Do not come near! Descend! *Hat Mage! Hat Mage!*
Shama	:	(Bewildered and hurt descends the stairs very upset.)
		Where should I go Baba. If you turn me away where should I go?

(SONG–DANCE 6: BABA AND THE SNAKE)

(Snake charmer music. Dancer dressed as a snake moves hypnotically and threateningly engaging Baba in symbolic combat. Ends with the defeat of the snake.)

(Shama makes gestures of being well and cured; and hugs Baba's feet.)

(Curtains Close)

ACT V:

SABKA MALLIK EK

Scene I: *Ramnavami* and *Urs*

(Baba in the masjid preparing for prayer and reciting the *Al-Fatih* and doing the muslim prayers. Abdul Baba is with him.)

>Bismillâh ir-rahmân ir-rahîm
>Al-hamdulillâhi rabb il-âlamîn
>Ar-rahmân ir-rahîm
>Mâliki yawm id-dîn
>Iyyâka na`budu wa iyyâka nasta`în
>Ihdinâ s-sirât al-mustaqîm
>Sirât al-ladhîna an`amta `alayhim
>Ghayr il-maghdûbi `alayhim wa la d-dâlîn

Translation

In the name of God, Most Gracious, Most Merciful.
Praise be to God, the Cherisher and Sustainer of the world;
Most Gracious, Most Merciful;
Master of the Day of Judgment.
Thee do we worship, and Thine aid we seek.
Show us the straight way,
The way of those on whom Thou hast bestowed Thy Grace, those whose (portion) is not wrath, and who go not astray.

Baba : There is only one God and He is Omnipresent.

There is only one Religion; the Religion of Love.

There is only one Caste; the Caste of Humanity.

There is only one Language; the Language of the Heart.

(Abdul Baba writes what he hears. He repeats diligently.)

Baba	:	(indulgently) Abdul... you and Hemadpant... what will you do with all this writing... may God increase your understanding... the *qalb* is the true page upon which is written the word of Allah.
Abdul	:	Baba, with your permission I have completed the cleaning of the masjid early this morning, the courtyard has been swept... what remains is the inner room... (pointing to the room around). Teach me more.
Baba	:	Abdul, you are wise... clean the courtyard well... for it is here that evil as well as good enters. We begin with the outer *maqam* always.
Abdul	:	(puzzled) Baba, I mean the Dwarkamai, here... the *safai*...
Baba	:	Aah, Abdul you speak of the external masjid, I speak of cleansing the internal masjid, the heart... who understands these words... clean it well Abdul... safeguard the fortress... watch it well — *sadr, qalb, fu'ad, lubb*... this heart is the seat of Allah... it is not easy. This masjid is where the *muwahhid* has his abode... the *al-nafs al-mut ma'innah*. The abode of unity is here... Ek.
		(changing expression, in tones of caution) Beware Abdullah... the smoke... always beware of the smoke... don't let it enter... clean it well... the *nafs* is sly and enters unseen.
		Be prepared Abdul. Be prepared for Allah. *Safai kar*... the guest comes unannounced. He is the real teacher who will finally grant you *al-haq iqah* ... only Allah can grant you

	the final reality... It cannot be learned from books or from a teacher.
	Allah Mallik!
Abdul :	Baba, what fear shall I have when you are here to guide me. He bows and touches his heart. Baba, did you hear? That Ramaswami converted to our Islam.
Baba :	That fool! Fools all! What is the need to change one's father, eh Abdul? He exists on all paths. Can one change one's father and mother like footwear? However fancy the design, footwear serves one purpose. Keep to one's own path and trust the *Sadguru* to take you across. One must never forget *Maruti*, he showed us what faith is. One should have faith like Maruti. My Allah asks for two things — like a shoe on each foot, Shraddha and Saburi take us to him.
Abdul :	Baba, this Dwarkamai is truly the abode of unity... today we will again see Musslaman and Hindus side by side in Shirdi. Rahim and Ram live together in this masjid. Baba, where else is our masjid called by a Hindu name. Where else is the abode of Allah, the father called *mai*, our mother... truly Baba, this is the abode of compassion. This Shirdi knows we can come to you for anything.
	Nana and others will be here soon to begin the Ramnavami preparations and I hear Chand Patil is coming too from Dhoop village for the Urs. (He bows with his hand on his heart and takes the broom and begins to clean the masjid.)

Radha	:	(Arrives with all other woman and kids. Some are holding a couple of vessels.) Baba, *pranam*... where should we put up the cradle? (Begins to help Abdul with the cleaning.) (Women begin decorating the masjid with *puja thaali* and flowers. Kids make rangolis.)
		(Lakshmi enters with *roti* and buttermilk for Baba and gives it to him.)
Lakshmi	:	*Chaas* Baba, and your roti.
Baba	:	I will remember your service well, Lakshmi beti. Year after year you feed me unforgetting of my needs.
		(Arrive Muslim men and women with ornate fabric, plates of sandal offering and incense. Bow to Baba.) Baba, we are ready for the Urs.
		(Arrive Mahalsapati, Hemadpant, Das Ganu, Chand Patil, Nana Chandorkar and all others with flags.) (All greet Baba. Both parties embrace and greet each other. Compliment each others' clothes and have general chit chat.)
Nana	:	Our Ram is here. (Gives a doll of Shri Ram to Radha Bai) (She puts it in the cradle.) (Children flock to the cradle.)
		Baba Pranam. Your Uddhi arrived in time. Naina has delivered safely.
Baba	:	Nana... I have been waiting for you. Is Naina *beti* well? The things I do for my devotees. Sometimes I have to even become a *tangewallah*. (laughing). Are you comfortable? Where are you staying?

Nana	:	Baba, the devotees are spread out in the *wadas*... Sathe wada and Dixit wada. All is well. All are comfortable. Some will visit the holy site of the neem tree and come here. Everyone goes to see the *padukas* now.
Shama	:	And the Sathe Wada. Ever since Baba asked Megha in his vision to draw Lord Shiva's trishul there are a stream of devotees now in the wada too. Megha still wonders how Baba appeared to him next to his bed when the doors of the wada were closed. He has carefully saved the *akshata* Baba threw on him.
Baba	:	(Smiling) I require no door to enter. I always live everywhere and carry on as a wire-puller.
Chand Patil	:	Baba! (he goes upto him) How many years it's been Baba!
Baba	:	Ah Chand Patil... How can I forget you? You escorted me to my Shirdi. (with a mischievous look) Any more horses on their way to **Aurangabad**?
Chand Patil	:	I would lose my all for you Baba. *Aap to hamara Avaliya hain. Allah ki nishaan hain.* You bring fire and water from the earth. *Duniya aapke unguliyon peh naachati hain.*
Baba	:	*Na Chand. Allah Mallik hain. Main bas unka das hoon.*
Baba	:	Ah Tatya, you wear a new turban. Suchi, come here, let me see your new *parkar*... And you, Lakshmi... you will be ready to be a bride soon. Kanha, you will dance

today, won't you? Vijju, here is sugar candy for you.

(The kids flock to him.)

Hemadpant, come here. Drink this buttermilk.

Hemadpant : I need to save my appetite for the feast later on. No Baba.

Baba : (gently cajoling him.) Go on you won't have this opportunity again. Accept what comes to you from this hand.

(Hemadpant drinks it).

Baba : Who knows Hemadpant? You may provide nectar after this that will give solace to all my *yaaran*... (laughing).

Bayyaja : (enters with naivadya) Baba, naivadya is here for Ram. Lakshmi beti, take this upstairs.

(Enter drummers) (Enter sword fighters)

(A peaceful procession of Ram Navami & Urs happens. Both parties proceed together out of the masjid and around the village. Drummers. Dancing. Music. A procession of Ram and Sita idols. Cries of *Jai Shri Ram*! Entire village participates, poor and rich alike.)

(Meanwhile, Baba is seen cooking in big *handis* and stirring the food with his bare hand.)

Das Ganu sings a kirtan in the procession.

(MUSIC/SONG DAS GANU KIRTAN)

Composed By: Shri Dasganu Maharaj

Shirdee maajze Pandharapura Saibaba Ramaavara
Baba Ramaavara, Sai Baba Ramaavara

Shuddha bhaktee chandrabhaabagaa, Bhaava pundaleeka jaagaa
pundaleeka jaagaa. Bhaava pundaleeka jaagaa

Yaa ho yaa ho avaghe jana karaa Babaansee vandana.
Saisi vandana karoo Babaansee vandana

Ganu mhane Baba Sayee. Dhaava paava maajze aayee
paava maajze aayee. Dhaava paava maajze aayee

(The kirtan leads the procession around the village and ends with a return to the masjid. The Hindu procession returns too saying Jai Ram. Rock the cradle.)

(The Urs procession returns to the masjid and the contents of the plate are thrown on the masjid walls with Baba's blessings.)

Shama : Baba, the *Qawalli* troupe is on its way and will be here soon. We must serve the Naivadya.

(Women spread out the leaves in two rows.)

(Baba is seen serving food lovingly while enquiring each one's needs.)

(Curtains Close)

(Curtains Open)

Scene II: Qawalli

(SONG-DANCE 6): QAWALLI

(Villagers are patting their bellies in contentment and remarking on the food.)

(Enter Qawalli singers)

(All settle down for the performance of one of Kabir's poems adapted to Qawalli)

Avadhuta Yugan Yugan Hum Yogi
Avayna Jay Mitaina Kabahun, Sabad Anahat Bhogi
Subhi Thor Jamat Humri, Sub Hi Thor Pur Mela
Hum Sub May, Sub Hai Hum May, Hum Hai Bahuri Akela
Hum Hi Sidh, Samadhi Hum Hi, Hum Mauni Hum Bole
Rup Swarup Arup Dikhake, Hum Hi Mein Hum Toh Khelen
Kahe Kabira Jo, Suno Bhai Sadho, Nahi Na Koi Icha
Apni Madhi Mein Aap Mein Dolu, Kheloon Sahaj Swa-Icha

Chorus:

Bin Sat-Guru Nar Rahat Bhulana

Translation:

Oh unattached being! I am a yogi from many a eons
I don't come or go nor do I get erased
I relish and enjoy the un-struck *Anahat Shabad*
In every direction I see only a collection and carnival of me
I am in everybody and everybody is in me. I am utterly alone
I am the *Siddha*, I am the *Samadhi*
I am the one who remains silent, I am the one who speaks
The form is my own form manifesting the formless
I am the one who plays with himself

Kabir says, listen Oh Sadhu! there is no desire anymore

I am floating in myself in my own little hut playing effortlessly by own desire.

(This chorus is the tile of another poem but would be appropriate as a chorus repeat here.)

(Baba is seen dancing in a trance.)

(Curtains Close)

ACT VI:

EK

Scene I: I do not feel well here

Radha Mai : (to Abdul) Abdul Baba. You were always warning me. I should not have let that *Phasle* clean the masjid. He broke that brick. It is my fault.

Abdul : Baba wept like a child yesterday Radha Mai. "It is not a brick but my companion that has been broken, *Sobat Tutali*," he said. "It was dear to me as my life. My luck and my fate."

Baba : (breathing heavily) You need not worry. Why do you take responsibility for your actions Radha Mai? You are not the doer. I too am at the mercy of my Mallik. All things have a certain life span. All things are transient.

Radha Mai : Baba, the *Dusshera* celebrations have begun. People are making merry. There are throngs daily in the Khandoba temple.

Bhagoji : Tatya, is not getting better. People are afraid that he may not last.

(In the background, in a dim light an ailing Tatya is seen lying in bed.)

Baba : Tatya is mine, Bhagoji. I told him so yesterday. At first I got two cradles for both of us, but now I've changed my mind. I don't want to take him now. I've changed my mind. I am going alone. (Struggling with breath) Nana, send this money to Shamsuddin for moulu, nyas and qawalli.

Nana : Baba, your asthma is getting worse. Why will you not let us bring you the doctor from Rahata? We beg you to stop your begging rounds for a few days.

Baba	:	No Nana. Allah is the only doctor I need. Call Vagne. Ask him to come with Rama Vijaya.

(Nana leaves and returns with Vagne.)

Read Vagne. Read… read to me of my Rama…

(Vijaya can be heard reading of Rama. Baba listens with a peaceful smile.)

Vagne	:	*And then, with unerring aim, aimed four arrows and killed the horses of Ravana. The demon-king replaced the horses. Rama aimed the half moon arrow that glinted with silver light. Ravana cut it off with his own. Whereupon, Rama let off one of his most powerful weapon gifted to him by the Gods, which struck the chest of the demon-king and cut off his ten heads. But lo behold! The heads fixed themselves to the torso of Ravana. It happened again and again. The vanaras despaired. All began to give up hope. The charioteer Matuli, said to Rama, "Ravana has got a phial of nectar in his breast. Break it and you will be successful!" Rama discharged the powerful weapon called Agasti Data — a weapon that makes the Gods tremble. The phial broke and immediately after, he cut off his ten heads and killed him on the spot.*

(Curtains Close)

(Curtains Open)

(Shama, Lakshmi Bai, Bhagoji, Nana, and all villagers are seen in the masjid.)

Baba	:	(in a weak and breathless voice) Go! Go! Go all of you. Go. It is the lunch hour.

A most fortunate day. *Vijaydashami*. Return to your families. Dine and return.

Shama	:	We will go after they return. (Most of the crowd leaves) (Shama and Nana sit down on the steps.)
Lakshmi	:	Haan Baba. We will remain with you. (Lakshmi Bai sits down on the steps as well.) (Baba struggles to an upright position and leans on Bhagoji. Bhagoji massages his shoulders.)
Baba	:	Lakshmi beti come here. Come here. (Lakshmi goes up to him from the steps.)
Lakshmi	:	Baba (goes up to him reverentially) what do you need Baba?
Baba	:	Come. Come. (He put his hand in his pocket and takes out five coins.) Here. One. Two. Three. Four. Five. Wait. I am not finished. (He puts his hand in his pocket again and gives her four more.) Six. Seven. Eight. Nine. (He places his hand on her head and blesses her.) I do not feel well here. Take me to the Degdi wada. I will be well there. I am going. Take me to the wada. (While saying these last words he leans on Bhagoji and breathes his last breath.) (As the light in Tatya's room brightens, the light in the Masjid is extinguished.) (Curtains Close)

Scene II: *Sabka Mallik Ek*

(Enter Baba holding Tatya and Lakshmi on either side.)

Baba : *You need not go far, or anywhere in search of Me. Barring your name and form, there exists in you, as well as in all beings, a sense of Being or Consciousness of Existence. That is Myself. Knowing this, you see Me inside yourself as well as in all beings. If you practice this, you will realise all pervasiveness and thus attain oneness with Me.*

My mortal remains will speak from My tomb. I shall be active and vigorous even from my tomb. My tomb shall bless and speak to the needs of my devotees.

If you look at Me, I look at you. This is my eternal promise to you.

Remember this well:

Tatya & (The three together say):

Lakshmi : *Om Sama Sarva Mata Muurtaye Namah! Sabka Mallik Ek!*

(Curtains Close)

Scene III: *Ek. Ek. Ek.*

(SONG-DANCE 7):
Title: (Ek. Ek. Ek.)
Oneness of religions dance
(With *Kaakad Aarthi*)

(Backdrop: Shadow play: The merging of various Gods into the merging of the village of Shirdi into Maharashtra into India into Earth into Milky Way into the Galaxy into Sai's form into one point of light.)

Na hi deeware, Na hi talwaare
Na hi bediyaan, Na hi batwaare

Sabka suraj ek
Sabka aakaash ek

Hum or tum bus shabde hain
Desh aur vesh bus maya hain

Sabka sthaan ek
Sabka praan ek

Na koi mantra, Na koi japa
Na koi yoga, Na koi Roza

Sabka mallik ek
Sabka ishwar ek

Mita de Mita de sab mita deh
Naam, roop, moh mita de

Sabka antara ek
Sabka Allah ek

Yahin hai jannat, Yahin nark ho
Apne aap ko uthao aur sambhalo

Sabka sadguru Ek
Sabka Sai Ek

Andhera mitado, Roshni jagaado
Hamdard sikhao, Pyaar hi pyaar karo

Yahin hai haj, yahin hai thirthyatra
Pehchanlao apne aap apni antaratmaan

Sabka antara ek
Sabka Allah ek
Sabka Rama ek
Sabka Sai ek

Humara sadhana, Humara Aradhana
Humara khushiyan, Humara shraddha

Pandurang Sai Dataa Sai Isai Sai
Allah Sai Akkalkot Sai Krishna Sai
Rama Sai Maitreyi Sai Siddharth Sai
Vallabha Sai Venkatesh Sai Ishaan Sai
Mallik Sai Shiva Sai Lakshmi Sai
Yehwah Sai Yama Sai Ishwar Sai Devi Sai
Sai Sai Sai Sai Sai Sai Sai Sai Sai Sai Sai

Ek Ek Ek

(Freeze)

(Curtains Close)

Glossary

Akshata	turmeric coated rice used in puja (Hindu rituals)
Anahat Shabad	the primal sound of the universe that is self-existing, uncaused, limitless and unceasing
Annadaan	free food offering
Chaacha	uncle (father's brother)
Chaas	buttermilk
Chillum	a short clay pipe used especially for smoking cannabis
Choli	short-sleeved blouse or bodice
Dargah	mausoleum; burial site of Muslim saints visited as pilgrimage sites
Darshan	beholding a Saint
Dhuni	sacred fire
Dusshera	Hindu festival celebrating the Goddess in the Hindu autumn lunar month
Fakir	Muslim or Sufi wandering holy man
Handis	deep, narrow mouthed cooking vessels
Kirtans	Hindu prayer songs that praise and glorify gods and goddesses

Kolamba	cooking pot; red, coarse kind of grass used for thatching
Leela	divine play
Loka	in Hinduism, the Universe or any particular division of it
Maaqam	rank or position
Masjid	mosque
Mussalman	follower of Muslim religion
Nafs	comparable to vasannas; the egoic self; distortions in the psyche that divide man from his divinity
Naivadya	food first offered to God before consumption.
Padukas	sandal or slippers of saints often revered as an object of worship
Puja thali	a plate that is used to hold prayer offerings
Qalb	heart; one of the dimensions of the heart in Sufism
Qawalli	Sufi/Islamic devotional songs sung in praise of the Allah
Rangolis	traditional decorative designs made on floors during Hindu festivals
Roti	Indian bread
Saburi	patience and perseverance
Sadguru	more than just a spiritual master; highest in the hierarchy of teachers.
Safai	cleanliness
Shraddha	faith
Vanaras	monkeys

Vijayadashami	Tenth day of Dusshera; a day of celebration. According to the myth that the Goddess vanquishes evil
Wadas	lodges
Yaaran	friends

The Writing of *Ek*

The writing of *Ek* is a mystery that I try not to unravel too much. I occasionally read the Sat Charitra for a friend or family whom I felt was in need and always noticed that things shifted within that week. My faith was not single pointed. I was not involved with the Austin Sai temple on any level. The Shirdi Sai magic began quietly and surely. On Guru Purnima day (July) of 2009 two original pictures of Sai came to me. I was unaware that it was Guru Purnima and that the pictures were to reach me. Later, that evening when a friend informed me that it was Guru Purnima, I realized that something significant had occurred.

In November 2010, a stray thought crossed my mind. Had the life of Sai been depicted as an English theatrical production? Wouldn't this be a wonderful idea to reach a younger English-speaking audience. The thought became insistent. Between Nov and Dec 2010, I increased my daytime Sai temple visits, started obsessively watching the Sai serial, read five books on Sai's life and began to write *Ek* on December 5. The first draft was completed in 35 days on January 9. It flowed with ease and the barest editing. I wrote sometimes in front of Baba's picture in my *puja* room. My personal relationship with Baba evolved during that process. *Ek* is probably the first English musical on his life in the world; a literary landmark. I felt the task given to me by Baba would be complete upon publication of the play. The book reaches a wider audience and can be staged anywhere. The premier musical production of *Ek* is slated for February 2012 in Austin, Texas where I live.

Baba gets you by the hook of your personality and temperament. I am a poet and he caught me through writing. *Ek* is not a product it is a process and a *sadhana*. My inner journey toward Baba is 'Ek' — my inner union with him. I lead a rather quiet life as a poet, a fairly fulfilling one — some international travel, readings for the Sahitya Academy and other landmarks; enough to assuage the feeling of personal success. And also enough disappointments to keep my ego in check as well! *Ek* has propelled my life in a completely new direction drawing many people into my life. The blessings and miracles have been many; too many to enumerate here.

There is very little we do for God and the writing of *Ek* was my service to the divine. I have not sought anything personal in this project or any commercial gain. We have pledged any profit from the first production in Austin to the Shirdi Sai temple's auditorium project. *Ek* for me was a vision. I saw a community of people emerging, gradually offering what they could give in service to the divine — talent, help, money, moral support and good will. It is exactly happening that way. *Ek* is not a play but a process of surrender that can bring people together with the quiet training of how to give with a spirit of service. Many people are working across the globe in the vision of global unity — a feature that is becoming more insistent in the last few decades in every sphere of human activity. Baba's overriding message and meaning of his presence on the planet was the message of oneness. He said his religion was Kabir's — a melding of paths and religions, transcending them while absorbing them.

I am keenly aware that Baba is peddled as a God who fulfills desires and performs miracles. God is under no obligation to prove his existence with miracle working. When it is done, it is the kindness of the divine to strengthen faith. Baba said so few came to him for the real treasure he had to give — inner spiritual training. He is badgered for the fulfillment of desires; our assessment of God is reduced to his ability of fulfilling our desires! Very few of us ask what can we do for God out of love for him? Some of God's greatest devotees undergo lives that are excruciatingly painful. Not many of us have the ability to take on that training. Baba's life was one of renunciation. The greatest spiritual figures that have made a lasting impact on the hearts of human beings were aligned with simplicity and bare material wants. All of us, in this incredibly material age, carry some sort of convenient personal equation — personal needs paired with calculated and comfortable surrender. When in Kashi we surrender the fruit we don't like. Sai works because he fulfills our desires!

My heart tells me eventually a deeper faith exists wherein these signs/miracles are no longer sought or trumpeted. There is always the trap of the ego on the path of personal miracles, feeling singled out or spiritually superior. For some genuine seekers, miracles occur naturally and are not sought. As the gap becomes smaller between the self and God, divine laws begin to operate. A few destinies unfold from this level. Every human being is somewhere on this timeless journey to God. I have many moments of weakness in a developing faith. I need proof and assurance at times. I cannot presume to have 100% faith. One such miracle has bearing here.

A few months ago I was racked by the question — had *Ek* really transpired with Baba's will? I have experienced effortless literary outpourings, so what was the guarantee that this was indeed Baba's work. I began to pray one evening for an answer to the writing of *Ek*. I asked for a sign that I could understand. After meditating, I thought of reading some literature about Baba. I randomly picked up a book on Sai by Antonio Rigopoulos, (a book of nearly 500 pages) opened a page and began reading. The para I read was about Sai giving his permission to the writing of the Sat Charitra. Of all the books I had, of all the pages and paras, how had I opened to an incident that had a direct bearing on my question? From that moment onwards I have worked for *Ek* without questions.

I am grateful to Sterling Publishers for acceptance of the manuscript. Mr. Ghai worked with me in a spirit of dedication to Baba. The Austin production in February 2012 will complete the vision and may herald *Ek's* journey into the world of theatre.

September 2011   **Usha Akella**

Our books on Shirdi Sai Baba

Shirdi Sai Baba is a household name in India as well as in many parts of the world today. These books offer fascinating glimpses into the life and miracles of Shirdi Sai Baba and other Perfect Masters. These books will provide you with an experience that is bound to transform one's sense of perspective and bring about perceptible and meaningful spiritual growth.

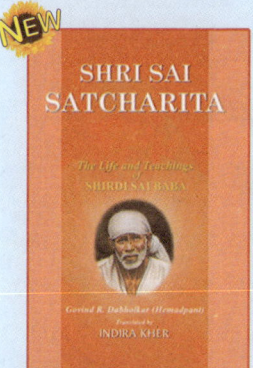

SHRI SAI SATCHARITA
The Life and Teachings of Shirdi Sai Baba
Translated by Indira Kher
ISBN 978 81 207 2211 8 ₹ 500 (HB)
ISBN 978 81 207 2153 1 ₹ 300 (PB)

Shirdi Sai Baba
Vikas Kapoor
ISBN 987 81 207 59701
₹ 30

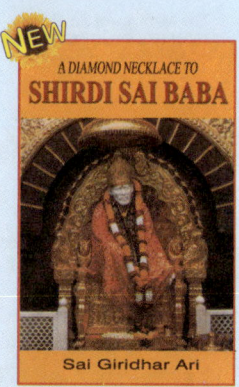

A Diamond Necklace To: Shirdi Sai Baba
Sai Giridhar Ari
ISBN 978 81 207 5868 1
₹ 200

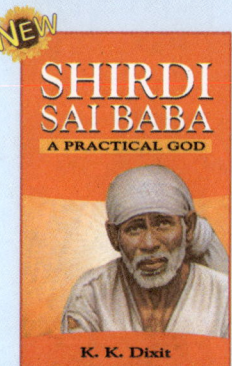

Shirdi Sai Baba
A Practical God
K. K. Dixit
ISBN 978 81 207 5918 3
₹ 75

The Eternal Sai Phenomenon
A R Nanda
ISBN 978 81 207 6086 8
₹ 200

Baba's Anurag
Love for His Devotees
Compiled by Vinny Chitluri
ISBN 978 81 207 5447 8
₹ 125

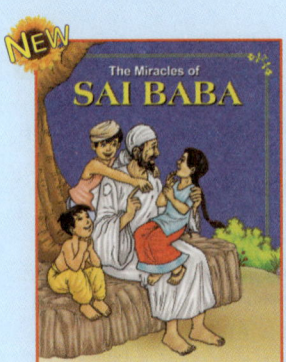

The Miracles of Sai Baba
ISBN 978 81 207 5433 1 (HB)
₹ 250

I am always with you
Lorraine Walshe-Ryan
ISBN 978 81 207 3192 9
₹ 150

Unravelling the Enigma: Shirdi Sai Baba in the light of Sufism
Marianne Warren
ISBN 978 81 207 2147 0
₹ 400

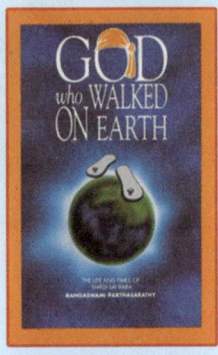

God Who Walked on Earth: The Life & Times of Shirdi Sai Baba
Rangaswami Parthasarathy
ISBN 978 81 207 1809 8
₹ 150

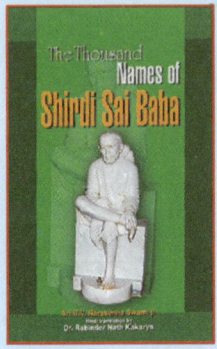

The Thousand Names of Shirdi Sai Baba
Sri B.V. Narasimha Swami Ji
Hindi translation by
Dr. Rabinder Nath Kakarya
ISBN 978 81 207 3738 9
₹ 75

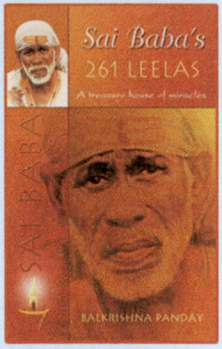

Sai Baba's 261 Leelas
Balkrishna Panday
ISBN 978 81 207 2727 4
₹ 125

108 Names of Shirdi Sai Baba
ISBN 978 81 207 3074 8
₹ 50

Spotlight on the Sai Story
Chakor Ajgaonker
ISBN 978 81 207 4399 1
₹ 125

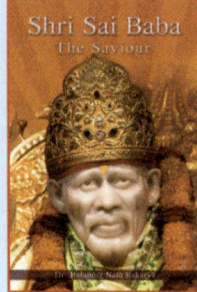

Shri Sai Baba-The Saviour
Dr. Rabinder Nath Kakarya
ISBN-978-81-207-4701-2
₹ 100

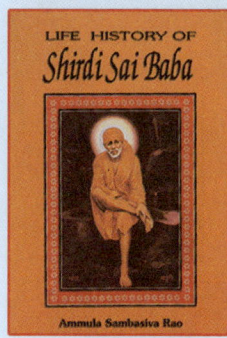

Life History of Shirdi Sai Baba
Ammula Sambasiva Rao
ISBN 978 81 207 2033 4
₹ 150

A Solemn Pledge
from True Tales of Shirdi Sai Baba
Dr B H Briz-Kishore
ISBN 978 81 207 2240 8
₹ 95

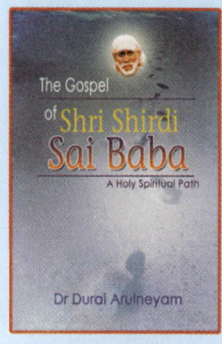

The Gospel of Shri Shirdi Sai Baba:
A Holy Spiritual Path
Dr Durai Arulneyam
ISBN 978 81 207 3997 0
₹ 150

Shri Shirdi Sai Baba: His
Life and Miracles
ISBN 978 81 207 2877 6
₹ 25

Shri Sai Baba's
Teachings & Philosophy
Lt Col M B Nimbalkar
ISBN 978 81 207 2364 1
₹ 90

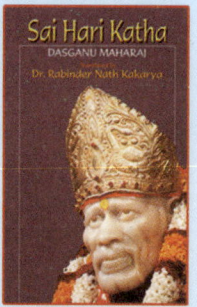

Sai Hari Katha
Dasganu Maharaj
Translated by
Dr. Rabinder Nath Kakarya
ISBN 978 81 207 3324 4
₹ 100

Sai Baba: His Divine Glimpses
V B Kher
ISBN 978 81 207 2291 0
₹ 95

Sri Sai Baba
Swami Sai Sharan Anand
Translated by V.B Kher
ISBN 978 81 207 1950 7
₹ 200

Shirdi Sai Baba and
other Perfect Masters
C B Satpathy
ISBN 978 81 207 2384 9
₹ 150

Baba's Rinanubandh
Leelas during His Sojourn in Shirdi
Compiled by Vinny Chitluri
ISBN 978 81 207 3403 6
₹ 200

Baba's Vaani: His Sayings and Teachings
Compiled by Vinny Chitluri
ISBN 978 81 207 3859 1
₹ 200

Baba's Gurukul SHIRDI
Vinny Chitluri
ISBN-978-81-207-4770-8
₹ 200

Shirdi Sai Baba
The Divine Healer
Raj Chopra
ISBN 978 81 207 4766 1
₹ 100

Sri Swami Samarth –
Maharaj of Akkalkot
N. S. Karandikar
ISBN 978 81 207 3445 6
₹ 200

Guru Charitra
Shree Swami Samarth
ISBN 978 81 207 3348 0
₹ 200

BABA- May I Answer
C.B. Satpathy
ISBN 978 81 207 4594 0
₹ 150

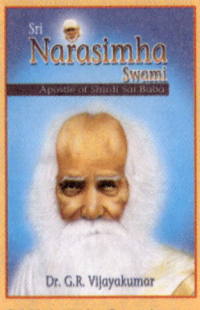

Sri Narasimha Swami
Apostle of Shirdi Sai Baba
Dr. G.R. Vijayakumar
ISBN 978 81 207 4432 5
₹ 90

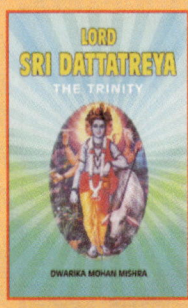

Lord Sri Dattatreya
The Trinity
Dwarika Mohan Mishra
ISBN 978 81 207 5417 1
₹ 200

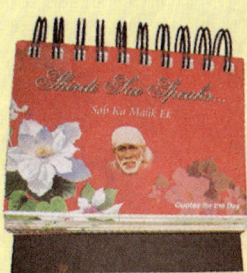

Shirdi Sai Speaks...
Sab Ka Malik Ek
Quotes for the Day
ISBN 978 81 207 3101 1 ₹ 200

शिरडी साईं के दिव्य वचन
सबका मालिक एक
ISBN 978 81 207 3533 0
₹ 180

बाबा का ऋणानुबंध
शिरडी में उनके तहवास के दौरान रची लीलाएँ
संकलन: विनी चितलुरी
अनुवादक: बेला शर्मा
ISBN 978 81 207 5998 5
₹ 125

शिरडी साईं बाबा
विकास कपूर
ISBN 978 81 207 5969 5
₹ 30

श्री साईं बाबा
के उपदेश व तत्त्वज्ञान
लेफ्टिनेन्ट कर्नल एम. बी. निंबालकर
अनुवादक: डॉ रविन्द्र नाथ ककरिया
ISBN 978 81 207 5971 8
₹ 100

श्री साईं सच्चरित्रा
डॉ रविन्द्र नाथ ककरिया
ISBN 978 81 207 2501 0 ₹ 250 (PB)
ISBN 978 81 207 2500 3 ₹ 300 (HB)

साईं शरण में
चन्द्रभानु सतपथी
ISBN 978 81 207 2802 8
₹ 150

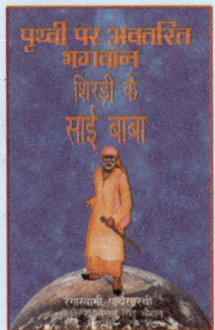

पृथ्वी पर अवतरित भगवान
शिरडी के साईं बाबा
रंगास्वामी पार्थसारथी
ISBN 978 81 207 2101 2
₹ 150

श्री साई बाबा के परम भक्त
डॉ रबिन्द्र नाथ ककरिया
ISBN 978 81 207 2779 3
₹ 75

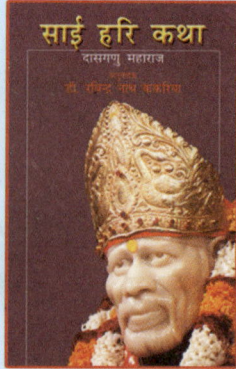

साई हरि कथा
दासगणु महाराज
ISBN 978 81 207 3323 7
₹ 65

साई—सबका मालिक
कल्पना भाकुनी
ISBN 978 81 207 3320 6
₹ 125

साई दत्तावधूता
राजेन्द्र भण्डारी
ISBN 978 81 207 4400 4
₹ 75

श्री शिरडी साई बाबा व अन्य सदगुरु
चन्द्रभानु सतपथी
ISBN 978 81 207 4401 1
₹ 90

बाबा आध्यात्मिक विचार
चन्द्रभानु सतपथी
ISBN 978-81-207-4627-5
₹ 100

बाबा की वाणी उनके वचन तथा उपदेश
बेला शर्मा
ISBN 978-81-207-4745-6
₹ 100

श्री नरसिम्हा स्वामी
शिरडी साई बाबा के दिव्य प्रचारक
डॉ रबिन्द्र नाथ ककरिया
ISBN 978 81 207 4437 0
₹ 75

शिरडी साई बाबा
प्रो डॉ बी एच ब्रिज़—किशोर
ISBN 978 81 207 2346 7
₹ 60

साई भक्तानुभव
डॉ. रबिन्द्र नाथ ककरिया
ISBN 978 81 207 3052 6
₹ 90

श्री साई बाबा के अनन्य भक्त
डॉ रबिन्द्र नाथ ककरिया
ISBN 978 81 207 2705 2
₹ 85

साई का संदेश
डॉ रबिन्द्र नाथ ककरिया
ISBN 978 81 207 2879 0
₹ 125

शिरडी संपूर्ण दर्शन
डॉ रबिन्द्र नाथ ककरिया
ISBN 978 81 207 2312 2
₹ 50

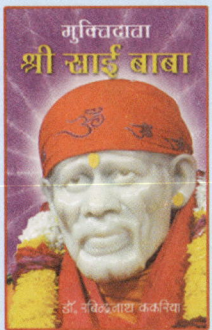
मुक्तिदाता श्री साई बाबा
डॉ रबिन्द्र नाथ ककरिया
ISBN 978 81 207 2778 6
₹ 65

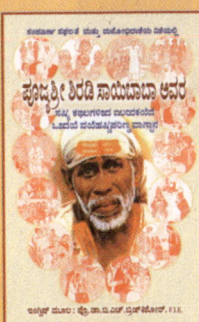
Shirdi Sai Baba (Kannada)
Prof. Dr.B.H. Briz Kishore
ISBN 978 81 207 2873 8
₹ 60

Shirdi Sai Baba (Telugu)
Prof. Dr.B.H. Briz Kishore
ISBN 978 81 207 2294 1
₹ 60

Shirdi Sai Baba (Tamil)
Prof. Dr.B.H. Briz Kishore
ISBN 978 81 207 2876 9
₹ 60

For detailed Catalogue visit our website
www.sterlingpublishers.com
E-mail:mail@sterlingpublishers.com